The Art & Science of Planning a Choral Concert

by
Barbara Harlow

Published by
Santa Barbara Music Publishing, Inc.
Post Office Box 41003
Santa Barbara, California, 93140

First Printing: July, 2011

Harlow, Barbara
The Art & Science of Planning a Choral Concert

ISBN: 978-0-9648071-7-4

As referenced in the book, the Choral Library Filemaker Pro database file
can be downloaded for free at www.sbmp.com. No restrictions are attached
to this item.

Thank You from the Author

To Geoff Lorenz for suggesting I write a book about
planning a concert.
To Anna Hamre for her program contribution
and enthusiasm about the book.
To Seth Houston for his careful read
and belief in the project.
To my son and co-worker David Harlow
for designing the cover
and patiently waiting for the project's completion.

The book is dedicated to my friend
Charlene Archibeque,
choral conductor extraordinaire.
Her inspired and well-planned concerts have, for many years,
been exemplary of what this book is about.

Foreword

Every choral concert has characteristics that are unique. Those concerts that are highly acclaimed are likely to feature an excellent conductor and to take place in a special location. In addition, these successful concerts will show evidence of much strategic planning.

Concert planning begins with the choice of literature. The music chosen will be the semester's curriculum, or, for the non-school group, the season's repertoire. Either way, the choices made will be the substance of many weeks of work. The concert, often being the driving force that dictates literature choice, must be carefully conceived. Ideally, its design will afford the opportunity for literature to be performed that has artistic merit, lasting value, a challenge appropriate for the ability level of the singers, and last but not least, audience appeal.

When planning a choral concert of several compositions, one needs to consider the "complete picture," the way the compositions fit together, much like a picture puzzle. The program should have form, various colors that complement each other, and above all a sense of style.

Science enters the picture when we consider acoustics as they apply to our specific concert needs. The physical structure of a venue, coupled with its acoustics, play a huge role in making or breaking a concert.

It is a science unto itself to figure out how to collect and keep track of repertoire. The filing cabinet, as storage unit, presents challenges: first to collect music to fill it; next to decide on a way to organize it; and finally to create a way to efficiently utilize it as a resource.

Planning a choral concert is not a simple thing. It is hoped that this book will guide, and make easier, the process from beginning to end.

Table of Contents

1
Your Personal Choral Library

Collect and Organize Your Choral Library

Choosing literature for a concert is a daunting task. It is made easier if the conductor has plentiful resources from which to choose. Ideally this consists of a filing cabinet loaded with single copies of music deemed worthy of performance.

There are numerous ways to discover literature to fill that filing cabinet. Here are a few:

> Subscribe to publishers' new issue services
> Attend reading sessions
> Attend choral concerts
> Join ACDA (American Choral Directors Association)
> Join Chorus America
> Attend the conventions of the above organizations
> Attend choral workshops
> Visit publisher websites
> Visit composer websites
> Become a frequent user of YouTube
> Read newspaper concert reviews
> Discover helpful online blogs
> Join discussion groups such as ChoralNet
> Buy recordings
> Search the music storage files where you work
> Browse the music bins of a music retailer

A conductor with an established account and a friendly relationship with a music dealer can readily order single copies of a list of titles. This same retailer, if they sponsor reading sessions, would likely agree to mail copies of these pieces to such customers if they could not attend a session. The retailer's goal is to sell music; to that end, they offer service.

With music in hand, it is time to get organized. The filing system needs to be decided upon. The choices are to file by...
  Title
  Composer
  Genre: title
  Genre: composer
  Voicing: title
  Voicing: composer
  Numerical

There is an advantage to sorting by genre. If planning a Christmas concert, all of the Christmas literature can easily be gathered from the filing cabinet; likewise, if filed together, all of the madrigals, or all of the spirituals, or all of the motets can easily be in hand. There is also an advantage to filing by title: if looking for a specific title, one needn't consider the genre, only the title. Another option is to assign a sequential number to each octavo, file the pieces numerically, and discover their location via a computer database.

After performing a piece, replace the score in the filing cabinet with your personal score, complete with your markings. Then if one day you choose to again use this title, some of your work is already done.

Recordings can also be "filed" for easy access. Put into operation the efficiency of the computer. Apple's iTunes, or Windows' Media Player, allow you to create folders to contain recordings of pieces you are considering performing. Now your recordings will be in one place. This is much more efficient than searching through a pile of CDs.

Some of your literature may be "filed" online. If both a viewable score and a recording are available at a website, you may not need a hard copy in your filing cabinet. How to keep track of these titles? Read on...

Create a Database

A computer database is a tremendous help in keeping track of any large body of information. FileMaker Pro is the most highly respected, and easiest to use, database program. It is available on a thirty-day trial basis, and is well worth the time to test it out. People use it to keep track of not just their music library, but also their book library, medical records, recipes, home repairs, addresses, trip planning, and as we will demonstrate in the appendix section, planning information and data regarding concerts.

When we address the issues of planning the concert, the value of the Choral Library Database will become self-evident as you sort it by title, or composer, or key, or genre, or when you wonder if you have a recording of a title. On the following page is a sample of what this database could track for you.

The Choral Library FileMaker Pro database is available as a free download at www.sbmp.com.

By adding fields of your choosing, the database can easily be altered to suit your special interests. The only caveat: after the thirty day trial period, you will need to buy the program in order to access the database. What you see on this page is a layout reduced in size. The data entered is for a piece referenced in this book.

date entered	5/6/2010
locater number	1
rating hot	☒ yes rating warm ☐ yes rating cold ☐ yes
title	Moon Is Distant from the Sea, The
composer	David Childs
arranger	
poet	Emily Dickinson
publisher	SBMP
catalog number	SBMP 719
language	English
country	U.S.
voicing	SSA
duration	3:40
key	D major
accompaniment	piano
range	moderate
difficulty level	medium
style	contemporary art song; great melody
mood	upbeat, pleasant
single copy filing location	drawer 1
online filing location	SBMP website
where discovered	SBMP website
single copy obtained from	new issue subscription
recording on file	Loughside Chamber Choir, Ireland, Judith Watson, conductor; at SBMP.com
possible uses	☐ Christmas ☐ closer other use [contest or convention] ☐ other holiday ☐ processional ☐ memorial ☐ encore ☐ opener ☒ large choir ☒ center piece ☒ small choir
date performed	5/9/2011
name of concert	Songs of the Earth and Sky
conductor copy on file	yes
number of copies on file	32
notes	Keep on file for use again; also available for SATB and TTBB - maybe perform a different voicing another time

Evaluate the Music

Your music judging ability will be well-served if you have a "measuring stick," a close relationship with the finest in music—let that be the "masters." Play a piano piece by Chopin, listen to a symphony by Brahms, attend concerts presented by the best professionals. Choosing music is rather like choosing friends—interesting friends enrich our lives. Keep the bar high as you choose music—let the greatest masters provide the yardstick.

When heard, the good piece creates some kind of emotional response. It has style, something that sets it apart and makes it special. It may have one element that is paramount, perhaps a beautiful melody, unique harmonic progressions, interesting rhythmic patterns, a dramatic climax.

Having decided you like the sound of the piece, consider the all-important matter of the text. Does the text have value unto itself? How would you describe it? Is it profound, inspiring, uplifting, obtuse, amusing? Given a good text, it should be obvious that the composer was not just inspired by it, but able to color the music so the text comes to life. On a technical level, look at the text in relation to the music. Are the accented syllables of words on strong beats? Are key words properly emphasized in the musical phrase?

Look at the piano accompaniment. It should evoke a style and be playable, supportive, and artistically interesting. It should not mainly be a copy of the vocal parts. Next check to see if the voice leading is technically correct—notes that need to resolve up or down do so. Leaps are not excessive. And very important, is "democracy" evident in the writing—does each part get a chance to shine? Pity the bass section whose only assignment in a piece is a drone. If this is a young group, good luck to the conductor trying to maintain order in the rehearsal room.

Music needs to be evaluated in relation to the choir that is to sing it. Are the ranges within reason? Is the difficulty level appropriate? Is there enough musical challenge to hold the interest of the singers for the length of the rehearsal span? Is the text one the singers will relate to or perhaps learn from? Last but not least, was the piece originally written to be performed by a small choir or a large choir? The piece written for a large cathedral choir will not be effective if a small choir is to perform it, especially if it is to be performed in an unfavorable, non-cathedral acoustic setting. The reverse also holds true. The delicate madrigal, composed to be performed in an intimate setting by a small group of singers, is likely to suffer when performed by a very large choir.

After all the issues are considered and you like the piece, what are its programming possibilities? Good pieces may have several possibilities: the opening piece for the concert, a theme piece, one with a meter that would work for a processional, the inspirational piece, the closing piece for the concert, the encore. Note all possiblities in the database

If you like a piece but it doesn't fit your present needs, file it for future reference. The crystal ball of a conductor cannot predict what kind of choral challenge may one day await them. The college director asked to direct a children's honor choir; the junior high director moving on to the high school; the church director moving to a school, or vice versa; the mixed voice choir director deciding to have the men and women of the group each do a composition alone; the conductor of a very large choir becoming the director of a chamber choir—if a piece is special, hang onto it.

2
Choose the Venue

Lucky is the conductor with a "home base" that includes a great performing venue. Very often this is not the case. Perhaps the only possibility is the school's tired multi-purpose room; or an acoustically dead, too-large auditorium; or a too-small, carpeted area in the church sanctuary. In these situations, if the opportunity to move the concert elsewhere becomes possible, let the search begin.

Acoustics

Dutch orchestral conductor Jaap van Zweden says of his favorite performing venue: "I don't care what concert hall I am at in the world, I want the sound of the Concertgebouw. The acoustic is always in my system. It's like a beautiful instrument."

When choosing a performance venue, the first consideration should be the acoustic properties of the building, the search for "the beautiful instrument." Singers sing better when they are blessed with good acoustics. They revel in the feedback the acoustics provide—their love of singing is fed by the sound. When the acoustics are dead, singers tend to struggle; hence they are not as expressive. The choir is much more likely to have tuning problems. All in all, performing where there are dead acoustics can be a humiliating experience for both the conductor and the singers.

Audiences are accustomed to hearing fine recordings through their ear phones, special speaker systems, at the movies with digital surround sound, or at live pop concerts, the sound amplified with reverb added. They immediately sense something is amiss if a choral group doesn't produce an engaging sound—their response is likely to be one of patient patronage.

An interesting science project would be to actually measure the reverb time of the hall you're considering. Engage the use of a stop watch with a second hand. Test the space using your own voice, or better, if there is a concert, attend, and time the sound reverb. In the case of the Santa Barbara Mission, you would find the reverberation time to be seven seconds. When choosing literature for a concert in this mission, this is an important consideration. Fast music will become a muddle; sixteenth century motets composed for cathedral acoustics will flourish. It is critical to know the acoustic makeup up of the venue before planning a concert. If a stop watch is not your style, simply talking loud, or offering up a song, will quickly let you know if the space would be suitable for a concert.

Typically, community auditoriums are built to be multi-purpose, taking into first consideration the orchestra that is to call the hall home. Many of these concert halls produce a clean and clear orchestral sound, but have very little reverb. If there is a hall anywhere built specifically for choral singing, I'd like to meet it! So we look on, and hope to find a space that is appropriate for what we do. If you can locate a hall with two or three seconds of reverberation, this is excellent. It will adapt well for choral performances of all styles of music.

Ambience
Having found a hall with appropriate acoustics, thereby taking care of the ears of the audience, now think about their eyes. It is special if your choice of venue has a perk that will enhance your program. Maybe a beautiful church, a hall with a history and some special character, maybe in a library or a museum. Note what the pros are doing: concerts in wine cellars, in the Roman Forum, in mansions, or in glass cathedrals. Look beyond the ordinary and you just might discover a unique place in your community open to your concert.

Size, Equipment, and Limitations of the Venue
Now to the ever-important practical side. Size needs to be carefully considered. There must be room for your singers to comfortably perform. A center aisle for a processional, and/or side aisles

to allow the singers to sing in the round—both can add greatly to the interest of a program.

If more than one choir is to be part of the program, the venue must be able to accommodate them. Carefully scrutinize the available space with an eye to how you would plan a concert.

Another part of the size equation is the number of audience seats. If you expect one hundred people to come to your concert, don't choose a venue with five hundred seats. Strive for a full house!

Is there a piano and perhaps an organ? If either or both are to be used, they need to be evaluated. Is the piano decent and in tune? Would you need to have one brought in, or pay to have the one tuned that is already there? Would you be allowed to do either? If need be, can you move the piano? If using the organ, what are the sight lines for the organist to see the conductor? Will there be other instrumentalists involved? Is there adequate space for them?

Additional questions about the venue include the following:
If it is a church, will this put a limitation on the kinds of repertoire you can perform?
Is the cost involved equitable?
Can you sell tickets at the door?
If desired, is there space available for a reception within the venue?
Is parking available?
Can you rehearse there?
If need be, will they allow you to bring in your own risers?
Is there a place for the singers to warm up, and one to securely store their belongings during the concert?

By now, you are probably exhausted from the thought of all this. You are not alone with this feeling. This is not an easy process. When deciding on a concert venue, nothing can be taken for granted and much must be considered.

Having found and secured the venue, develop good political skills with the in-charge person, and by all means, the custodian or stage manager. This person will be your aide in time of need. You and the performers are guests in this place. As conductor, keep this constantly at the forefront of both your thinking and your actions, and see that the performers do likewise.

Worthwhile venues will have contracts to be signed. Liability for any incurred damage will be yours to cover. Limitations on the use of the facility will be carefully spelled out. The performers need to be aware of any caveats related to the use of the building and its resources.

Due to the difficulty of finding a suitable place to perform, many choirs have annual concerts in one place, year after year. Perhaps a wonderful Gothic styled church has been found for a Christmas concert, one that invites a procession, allows candlelight, and has special ambience. A great concert in a special venue can do a lot to establish a reputation for a choir. Fortunate is the choir that can build a loyal following of people looking forward to the next opportunity to hear them in this special place.

As we choose literature for the concert, to a great extent the venue will dictate what can be performed. Therefore, very often it is important to work in reverse: have in mind the type of concert that is to be presented and choose a venue that will work for it.

For those of you that feel the need, but are denied a venue choice, do what you can to get the best acoustics and ambience possible in the assigned space. Adding a choral shell behind the singers can help. If a church has carpeting where the singers are to perform, see if it is possible to remove it. If you are a school conductor and nothing can improve a really bad situation, seriously consider educating the administration of your need to move the concert elsewhere. For the choral conductor working in a church with bad acoustics and performing space, consider moving to a different church!

3

Choose a Theme
And a Title

Leonardo da Vinci, the Italian renaissance artist, scientist, and inventor, famously said "Creativity is born of restraint and dies in freedom." A concert theme helps narrow the choices, avoiding the need to consider a vast array of literature. And it opens up creative possibilities for making the concert more interesting. While a theme needn't govern every title on a program, it should have enough impact that its presence is felt. The idea is to use the theme both to build the program, and to create interest in the concert.

In the business world, having a unique and clever title is a marketing necessity. Two examples are Apple and Netflix. These are valuable titles. Go to the Los Angeles Master Chorale website to see how this magnificent choir is titling their concerts. You will not see *Choral Concert* listed—instead, you will see some interesting titles. They have built a loyal audience through their creative programming. If this great choir found the need to be imaginative with their concert titles, it behooves the rest of us to do likewise.

The concert title appears on the poster, the flier, the program cover, and the website. Sell the concert—that is the goal, be it one presented by children, collegiate, community, or professional singers.

Concert Titles
Six Centuries of Choral Music
This educationally sound concert title provides an opportunity to expose both the singers and the audience to a wide variety of literature. One needn't include something from every century, but the

span of the literature should encompass all six, starting with music from the sixteenth century and moving up to present day literature.

A Festival of Song

This title is worthwhile because "festival" implies celebration. It could be changed to a seasonal title: A Spring or Winter Festival of Song. Any of these titles could be used annually. They offer both focus and freedom. These are especially good title choices if the program is to feature the entire vocal program of a school, including more than one choir, perhaps an outstanding vocal soloist, a barbershop quartet, and even an excellent instrumentalist who happens to be part of the choral program. The title has few limitations and opens the door to any and all comers.

Sacred Sounds

The title might seem to confine the scope of the music to sacred music, but that is not really the case. "Sacred" can be amplified to include nature, art, peace, or anything precious and endearing that comes to mind. If you have a wonderful church in which to perform, this could be an especially appropriate theme.

Love In Deed

This title was created by Ken Berg for his May, 2011 benefit concert in Birmingham, Alabama, the state having been ravaged by destructive tornados. The concert, presented by three choirs, was given "to honor those whose lives were forever changed," and to raise money for Disaster Relief. When presenting a concert such as this, it is good to have a title other than simply *Benefit Concert.*

Songs of the Earth and Sky

David Childs' piece, *The Moon Is Distant from the Sea*, could be the inspiration for this title. Many pieces have been set to texts about stars, rivers, the land, and the sea.

Alleluia

Alleluia is an expression of thanksgiving, joy, and triumph. There are many pieces with *alleluia* as part or all of the title, or that include an *alleluia* section in the piece. The opener of this program might be a chant, the final piece Ben Allaway's hugely celebratory *Alleluyah Sasa.* Other parts of the program could express joy in its many forms.

Life, Liberty, and the Pursuit of Happiness

A direct quote from the United States Declaration of Independence, this could be the title for a patriotic program. Or it might simply offer an inspirational theme, allowing for a variety of literature.

From Korea to Kentucky
From Tokyo to Tennessee

A geographic title could add a bit of interest to a program featuring multicultural music, the final location being "home."

Legacy of Leipzig
The Glories of Venice
Mars and Venus
Choristers and Other Critters

These concert titles were created by Anna Hamre, Director of Choral Activities at Fresno State University. *Mars and Venus,* planned for 2112, will feature masterworks for men and women. Appendix Four presents the program for the concert titled *Choristers and Other Critters.*

How Can I Keep from Singing
Wondrous Love
Rejoice!

The above three are titles of pieces in the SBMP catalog. Any one of them could be a title and theme for a program. Either of the first two of the group could work as the opening number of a concert, setting the tone for what is to follow. *Rejoice!* would do the opposite: it could be the closing number of the concert, the culmination of many pieces leading up to this dramatic concluding number.

With a Lily in Your Hand

Eric Whitacre's piece was the title of a 2011 concert presented by the New York City New Amsterdam Singers, Clara Longstreth, conductor. The piece concluded the first half of this program. The New York Times concert review stated "The concert had a dual theme: the first part of the program explored Romanticism and tone painting in recent American choral music; the second half focused on modern reconsiderations of folk melodies." The concert title alone created more than a bit of intrigue for this concert. A lily appeared on the poster and the program cover.

The Poem, the Song, the Picture
This concert title is borrowed from Terry Schlenker's composition which would be central to the concert program. It suggests an opportunity for a multi-media feature, with readings either by student or published poets, accompanied by relevant projected artwork.

Dancing Tree
Nancy Gifford's children's choral piece *Dancing Tree* might inspire a concert theme focused on elements of nature. It could also be an excellent choice for a concert that features both choral music and dance, not necessarily happening at the same time.

Animalia
Another children's choral piece, this one by Earl J. Reisdorff, the title would arouse curiosity and work beautifully for a concert that featured a group of pieces about animals—there are many of these written for children's choruses.

The Artistic Value of a Title
Good is the concert title that can lead to artistic renderings for the program cover, poster, and/or flier, and perhaps inspire something artistic that will decorate the performance space. This again caters to the eyes of the audience. As it does so, it adds a feeling of "special" to a performance. Los Angeles' Disney Hall has a music series titled *The Green Umbrella*. The name makes little sense until one goes to one of these concerts and sees above the open, uncovered stage, green umbrellas suspended from on high by their handles, with green spotlights illuminating them. The umbrellas create the feeling of a proscenium arch and define the center stage area where

often, for this series, a small instrumental group is featured. The mystique of the title is appropriate as the music performed on this concert series is new, extremely varied, and often quite esoteric.

A touch of something artistic that relates to the theme is a great addition to any program. Again, audiences come with both eyes and ears. The more the concert can stimulate their senses, the better. Green umbrellas hanging from the ceiling may not be your thing, but the thought of them might inspire something equally creative.

The Theme and the Singers

The type of singers in your choir, or choirs, plural, should be considered when choosing a theme. Obviously, not all choirs are created equal. What is it that your choir would excel at, relate to, learn from, and enjoy? It's up to the conductor to make the choral menu a meaningful one, worthy of the singer's time and effort and interesting enough that they will grow from the experience.

Is there an ethnic background predominant in the group that could lead to a unique theme? Is there a special singer, gifted in some way, that deserves the attention a concert spotlight might provide? The opportunity to bring all or part of the focus of a concert close to the hearts and souls of the singers is precious and well worth exploring.

4

The Musical Structure

The Concert Shape

A good concert has a shape. There is the "arc," a program that has a central piece that is longer and of great import to the program. It might include instrumental accompaniment, soloists, a reading, dancers, projections of pictures—something makes this piece special. It can be the axis around which the program operates.

Then there is the "slope," a program that gradually leads up to a spectacular ending. This concluding piece may be longer than all the others, or again, involve additional features beyond the singing.

Another shape might be likened to "ocean waves." This concert has pieces that contrast each other, with some waves being taller or wider than others.

Whatever the shape, it is important that there is one. The flat concert shape will lack in interest. It likely consists of many similar short pieces strung together with little thought other than getting them all sung on the program.

The Concert Opener

The opening piece of a concert should be welcoming and exceptional. Its assignment is to alert the audience that this is going to be a very special concert. It is hoped that it will remove them from the thoughts of all that has gone on in their day and focus them on the moment.

Roger Wagner extracted a small group from his large Chorale that did masterworks with the Los Angeles Philharmonic, and they concertized on their own. For these concerts he opened with what was known as his "signature piece:" Tomás Luis de Victoria's exquisite *Ave Maria*. Expert at conducting Latin motets, and blessed with highly capable singers, he was able to set the tone for the entire concert as listeners were entranced by this opening number.

Numerous singers have performed Ed Hughes' *Alleluia, Rejoice* as an opener for their Christmas concerts. Audience members have reported that it was their favorite part of the program. The arrangement involves handbells and is perfect for a procession, singing in the round, or both. It combines *O Come, Emmanuel* with the traditional *Hodie* chant. Another such piece that is great for spatial singing formations is Ross Whitney's *Pentatonic Alleluia*. It consists of layers of chants, all on the word *alleluia*. Audiences love it when the singers are out among them, particularly when this happens as the concert begins.

At the 2009 ACDA National Convention in Miami, the Incheon City Chorale from Korea stunned the choral director audience with their opening number. Sung in their native language, the piece was composed by a Korean. A few of the members came on stage and starting the singing, sans conductor, when suddenly, from far-off in the audience, a glorious solo soprano voice was heard. Soon she was joined by others from the chorale scattered throughout the hall. They made their way to the stage singing, all of them with gorgeous voices. The result was electrifying to the ears. The eyes, meanwhile, were treated to a variety of bright-colored traditional Korean outfits. The conductor, Hak-Won Yoon, last to enter the stage, was dressed in an especially dramatic garb. As an opener, this was captivating.

For a Montessori pre-school "short song" concert, the opener was simply the act of sixty little kids getting onto risers! Obviously carefully rehearsed in this procedure, this drew great applause when all these four-year-olds got into place. Getting singers onto risers needs to be thought of as part of the show. All eyes are upon this activity. If possible, especially with a large group, get creative, having two rows enter simultaneously, one from the right, the other from the left. On occasion, choirs have been known to enter from the wings singing. If there are stairs leading up to a stage, they might process in singing as they enter from the back of the auditorium. If the venue is a church or hall with no stage, the procession is a bit easier to achieve. Depending on the style of the music, a drummer might lead a procession, or a simple song flute, or a fiddler, borrowed from the cast of *Fiddler on the Roof.*

Do something special to set the tone of the concert. Beginnings are very important to the whole.

The Concert Closer

Audiences need a choral "present," something special to send them back out into the world. What is the feeling you'd like them to take home? Just as the Roger Wagner group had their opening piece, the St. Olaf Choir has a signature ending piece: *Beautiful Saviour,* arranged by F. Melius Christiansen. With many alumni in the audience, plus people that are loyal followers of this historic choral program, this nostalgic ending is truly a heart-warming gift.

If the shape of the program dictates that it peak at the end, the final piece has a double duty: it provides the farewell "present," plus it is to be the most impressive, important number on the program. Look at the ending of the piece, and ask if it does the job of "gifting" the audience. Such a piece is *Bandari,* by Ben Allaway. This African-themed composition is twenty minutes long, and ends with *Freedom Come,* a piece that has, by itself, ended many a concert.

Instead of one large piece, the program that peaks at the end could feature a familiar group of pieces, such as arrangements of beloved folk songs and/or spirituals. Audiences are always pleased to hear a song they know and love dressed up in new garb.

The arc-shaped program may feature something at the end that relates to the beginning. If the choir sang their way into the concert, they could sing their way out. If they came in singing a madrigal, another madrigal might take them out the door. If the Christmas concert started with a familiar carol and a procession, it could end with *Silent Night*. The conductor might invite the audience to hum along on a final rendering of the piece, the choir also humming as they make their way to the door.

The final offering also could be the last piece in the puzzle relating to the theme of the program. Whatever the choice, this last piece needs to be as special as the first piece.

The Concert Middle

The audience is now warmed up to the choir and the program, so this can be the place for something more challenging. Compare it to a meal and it is the main course. If there is a theme to the program, several pieces could work together here to illustrate the theme. Or if the shape of the program is an arc, one longer composition could fulfill this duty.

A sacred concert might choose a Bach cantata for this spot in the program. In this case, the venue would need space for a small chamber orchestra. Another possibility is a short, a cappella mass. These are numerous and can be found in all eras of musical literature.

Ten to fifteen-minute secular pieces are not that plentiful. Easier to come by is a set of three or more pieces by one composer, or a group of pieces related to the theme by various composers.

The Art and Science of Finishing the Puzzle

You've discovered many pieces that will work for the concert. You've found a good opener and closer. Piecing all of this repertoire together takes much consideration, and some common musical sense. Some "rules" follow that will make your concert flow musically and artistically.

Avoid having two pieces sung in a row in the same key. Think as the composer does when writing a sonata, or a concerto, or a symphony. The movements relate in tonality. The second movement might be in a minor key, related to the major key of the first. Or it might be in the dominant of that key. It is amazing how organizing a choral program in this way can have a subtle but profound effect on a concert. It gives the concert cohesion and variety at the same time.

Do not have two pieces in a row in the same tempo. Back to the sonata form. Vary the tempos from piece to piece.

If the style of a piece is highly rhythmic, follow it with one with a great melody. Then do not follow that beautiful melodic piece with another great melody piece. Instead, have the next composition be one with an amazing harmonic structure. The idea is to have the neighboring pieces friendly with each other, but not competing. A composer writing a set of three pieces will follow these guidelines; each piece will be unique in tempo, key, and (to a degree) style, with the three related to each other.

The Los Angeles Master Chorale website eloquently describes their concerts: "Vintage Grant Gershon — with perfect pairings of great music — works that complement each other but have unique sonic imprints." It might not be a bad idea to post this concept on your music filing cabinet!

The Intermission

Some conductors like intermissions: their programs always include them. Others obviously do not. No doubt, in both cases, these conductors could provide good reasons for their thinking. "It breaks the mood" may well be one such reason for not having an intermission. Or, it could also be the reason for having one. If the concert was to take on a different character after an intermission, a break would make this change seem much less sudden.

The structure of a concert may dictate that an intermission is a necessity. If the last piece on a concert includes an instrumental ensemble, the intermission will provide the opportunity to set the stage for the instruments. Or it could allow a large choir to completely change their position on stage. If something was the visual decoration in the first half of the program and needed to be altered for the second half, the intermission allows this to happen.

If necessity is not the reason for an intermission, an opportunity for socializing for the audience, and a break from singing for the choristers, are other possible reasons. The audience steps out of the concert hall and has the opportunity to visit with friends, eat a cookie, or buy a CD. Meanwhile, the choir can tend to personal matters, a drink of water, or a slight change of costume. What the singers should not do is become one with the audience. It is best if they remain performers until the program is over.

The Encore

Like the intermission, some choose to have an encore and others do not. The encore under no circumstance appears on the printed program. But, for the conductor and the performers, it is to be thought of as an important part of the program. It is strategically chosen to be the "send home" piece. It typically follows a piece guaranteed to get a rousing ovation. It should not compete with such a piece, but instead, offer contrast. It should be short. And in some way, meaningful. A well-wisher of a piece. An "amen" to the concert. The encore could be the means by which the choir exits the building—they process out singing. The encore is a surprise. Audiences love pleasant surprises and feel rewarded by them.

The Commissioned Piece

Some choirs have the monetary resources to commission a new piece. It adds special excitement to a concert when a work is premiered, particularly if the composer is present to take a bow. And it is extra special for the singers if they get the chance to interact in rehearsal with the composer.

Composers will appreciate some guidelines and may reject some. If publication after the fact is their goal, they will wisely not choose to write something so esoteric it has little chance of getting published—for example, a piece requiring two oboes and a harp. From the conductor's standpoint, the request may fulfill a specific need for a thematic program or for a special type of piece to take on a foreign tour. Whatever the creation, the key to the success of the process is good communication between conductor and composer and a choir eager to be part of a world premiere.

5

The Physical Presentation

There are many aspects of the physical presentation to consider. We'll start with the most critical: the formation of the choir as it sings. There are as many variables here as there are sizes of choirs, types of venues, kinds of programs, traditions, and philosophical leanings of the conductor.

Staging the Large Choir

For a large choir, getting into place on the risers and staying there is pretty much the whole story. Therefore, the position in which the singers are positioned needs to be appropriate for the pieces chosen for performance. The wise conductor will experiment and see what works best for the makeup of the choir and the nature of the program.

Choices are:
Men on one side, women on the other
This works very well if there are an equal number of men and women. It is also works well if the music, which it often does, plays the men against the women.

Men behind the women
This accommodates height problems, as most men will be taller than the women. The sound of the men will not be quite as strong as when men are together on one side. However, if there is a shell behind the choir, this may correct the problem. One cannot know for sure without experimenting in the actual performance situation.

Men in the middle, women on the sides
At Disney Hall, the Los Angeles Master Chorale performed the

Brahms *Requiem* to great effect in this formation: S-B-T-A. There are an equal number of men and women in this very large choir. Occasionally you see this same arrangement when there are very few men. Placing them in the middle, and up front, can help balance the sound.

Man/woman alternated
Small choirs occasionally sing in this formation, but you rarely see large choirs doing this because this formation does not work well for all pieces. When the men or the women are featured musically, it is good for the audience to be able to focus their eyes on them as a group. It helps the audience understand the structure of the music. And, it is more efficient for the conductor—they can easily cue in a section as a group.

Large choirs in a large church could start a program singing in the round out in the audience. Then have a processional, singing their way to their places on risers. This is a dramatic way to open a program. But once on the risers, that's probably it for their placement until the end of the concert, or an intermission.

Staging the Small Choir
The venue has a lot to do with how the small choir is staged. If the performance is to be in an auditorium and the singing is to be from a stage, using risers is one option. If risers are used, it is good to have enough of them so the singers can spread out. The sound effect will be astounding. They will sound like a much bigger choir than when they stand tightly positioned together. And they will be able to hear each other better. The use of risers will, however, limit the movement of the choir. It is a bit awkward to change standing positions when risers are involved. If performing in a church using steps as the risers, the limitation is less. There may only be a couple steps, in which case moving to a new position becomes quite do-able.

The small choir with around twenty singers has many options for their formation, all of which can greatly enhance a program. Think of each piece as a picture. What standing position would work best for the singing of the piece? What standing position would best represent the musical structure of the piece? The following are some options:

Sing alternated, men and women. This can work well if the piece is harmonically intense. Jazz choirs sing this way in quartets, each singer carefully tuning their note of the chord with their neighbors.

If a piece has antiphonal or contrapuntal qualities, move the men to one side, women to the other. Many pieces, both serious and fun, have been written that feature a conversational effect between the men and the women. This standing position brings such pieces to life.

Sing in a circle. This is a novel approach, but for a complex piece, it works well for the singers, and can be fascinating for the audience as they watch the singers intensely interact.

Place a soloist out front of the group, the singers in a half-circle behind.

Start a song with the singers' backs to the audience. This is a mysterious thing to do. It can have a great effect if the song has a beginning that this would somehow enhance.

Scatter the singers over the entire performance area. The piece might be one that could be staged, as though it were part of a Broadway musical. It could be a gospel-style piece, or an upbeat spiritual, music that will be enhanced by visible physical involvement, and seem dead without it.

Embellish a piece with American Sign Language. *Silent Night* is beautiful signed.

Stage a madrigal setting. With dramatic aplomb, have two men bring in a table, others bring in chairs, the women set the table, put on the candelabra, and then some, or all of the group, sit down, and all sing a set of madrigals. If done with style, the set-up will be entertaining. The delivery of the madrigals then must live up to the mood established and continue the drama. Having created this physical set-up, no one wants to sit and watch it be taken down. So this is a good programming idea for the end of a concert, or for a set of pieces before an intermission.

As you can surmise, the possibilities for staging are endless. With a little imagination, the small choir can add great drama to their presentation via their staging, and sing better because of it.

Staging the Multiple Choir Concert

Many school conductors are faced with the necessity of presenting more than one choir in a concert. The challenge is to choreograph all movements so they are as seamless and efficient as possible. The momentum of a program will quickly die if there are large gaps while choirs enter or leave the stage. Careful and clever planning is needed to avoid this. Possibilities include the following:

Close the stage curtain. As it closes a small group or soloist appears in front of it. The show goes on. Meanwhile, behind the curtain, another choir is getting into position.

Have two choirs in view. One seated, listening, the other performing.

Each choir sings as they move in or out of the spotlight. Audiences love processions.

A soloist or small group performs as others move. Or, a small instrumental ensemble provides "travel music."

The venue will limit or enhance the opportunities for creating an interesting concert with multiple choirs. Hence, for the conductor with this challenge, the choice of venue is extra critical.

The Appearance of the Choir

The day of the choral robe for school or professional choir use is practically gone. Now, with a world of choices, this can be a painful subject for the choral conductor. It needs to be taken into consideration long before a concert.

Young singers dressed in the simplest way can look fresh and impressive. The goal is to make them uniform in their appearance. An all-white outfit is one possibility. A little touch of color can set the outfit off—a colorful sash, or a vest.

For more mature choirs, an often-used possibility is to rent tuxes for the men and provide the women with dresses from one of the many suppliers that specialize in outfitting choirs. Unless one has an willing dressmaker at hand, making dresses for the ladies of a choir can be a ponderous proposition. Another popular idea is the all-black approach. The men wear long-sleeve black shirts, black pants, and black shoes. For women, it's a black top, black long pants or a black skirt, and black shoes. If the skirt is short, the picture is complete with the addition of black nylons. Again, the addition of a touch of color can add some pizazz to these outfits.

Some choirs choose the costume approach: each singer wears something unique but all are dressed within a chosen theme. A concert focused on multicultural literature might feature outfits that represent the style of the various countries.

One very important detail to think about when perfecting outfits is again the venue. Stages afford a much more critical eye to the audience than does the church setting. Uniform shoe color becomes an important issue. And if the dresses are identical, uniform dress hem length, in relation to the floor, is a must.

Looking beyond outfits, many conductors suggest that the girls (and the boys!) comb their hair back from their faces. It's the face of the singer that the audience wants to see. Any extra additions to the hair should be discouraged, such as bows or ribbons or highly noticeable jewelry like hair-clips. The exception: everyone in the group takes on some of the look of a soloist. In this case, conductor beware: audition the "looks" before the concert.

The Appearance of the Conductor

Men, you are very lucky. Wear a good fitting, well-pressed black suit or tux, and black shoes with a high polish, (some prefer patent leather), and call it a day. You can now relax and stop reading for a moment, unless you happen to have a wife who is also a choral director.

Women: Reviewers have been known to review the outfit of the woman conductor. In the case of the Long Beach Symphony, the conductor wore tennis shoes! The reviewer didn't mention if they were black. One could hope they were. The Santa Barbara Symphony, for several years, had a woman conductor. On occasion, her outfits inspired comments in the local paper. As concert attendees and wives of orchestra players, a friend and I played fashion police, and rated her outfits on a scale of one to ten. When it was a ten, we made a point of telling her how wonderful her outfit looked. When a one, we simply felt sorry for her.

Finding your performance outfit can be quite the project. First consider the look of the women in your choir. If they have a simple, unadorned look, it is inappropriate for the conductor to come out looking very high-style. Let the style of your outfit not match that of the singers, but complement it. If it is a bit flashier than theirs, okay. But be careful, this is not about making a big fashion statement; it's about good taste.

It is highly recommended that you take a style-conscious friend with you when you go shopping for your concert outfit. More important than the front view is the rear view. Raise your arms, move them about. What does this do to the outfit? Is it at least as becoming on you from the rear as the front? And, take a cue from the men in their suits: When arms are waving, long sleeves are preferred. Check your mirror for validation of this.

A book of pictures of women conductors could be a very amusing thing—and quite a negative record. Many fail dismally on this issue. Personally, I was fortunate to not only have a mother with keen and critical eyes, who was an excellent seamstress, but also a close friend who owned a fashion boutique and had expert opinions on what looked good. Between the two of them, my outfits got the once over, and if need be, alterations to get the hem straight despite my uneven hips. Needless to say, I guarded my few performance outfits carefully. One year on December fifth, a brush fire threatened our home and we had to suddenly evacuate. I had little time to take anything along. What did I put in the car? My special outfit for the December Christmas concert.

Movement that Enhances the Performance

Television and YouTube have made it possible for people everywhere to both see and hear many types of performances. Visual has become an important part of the performing equation. That said, the traditional approach is still alive and well. The choir stands majestically in place and sings the entire concert sans movement. This is a powerful thing if the choir is number one, excellent, and number two, very large. The sheer impact of the size of the Mormon Tabernacle Choir is sufficient to wow any audience. The smaller choir can take a different approach. They have the option to include some type of group movement to enhance their performance.

It has been demonstrated over and over at choral conventions where many choirs perform that a little bit of action, added with great taste and élan, can be the spice that makes a performance both fun and memorable. After listening to a choir beautifully sing several pieces, it is refreshing to see them suddenly come to life at some point in a song, moving as a group to emphasize an aspect of the text or the music. This often will happen during the final piece of a program. The dessert. Done earlier in the program, it will establish a need to continue to include some kind of movement—once action is introduced to the audience, it is anticipated.

Any kind of group movement needs to be carefully rehearsed to achieve uniform perfection. The most common movement is clapping, something most any size choir can do. Usually it occurs because the composer included clapping as an element of a piece. Sometimes, without this direction, it is added to enhance the performance. Whatever the case, let it be stylized to match the nature of the piece. If Spanish, look to flamenco dance for the style. If gospel, African, or American folk, each has its own definitive style—discover it and put it to dramatic use.

Sometimes movement is something as simple as changing the focus of the singers, a move that captures the moment. If the men are singing a brief section of a piece that interests the women, and the women turn and look toward them, it creates a dramatic impact. This powerfully focuses attention on the meaning of the song. Turning back to face the audience, the women might then get their turn to be the stars, the men turning to watch them. A little show business can do a lot to build interest in a concert.

Show business aside, some conductors encourage their singers to move individually, as soloists, while they sing. These singers are not crowded together. They have room so their arms can move at will, their bodies not frozen in place, but free to move within a small zone of space. The musicality level of these performances is often top-notch. The singers are very in touch with the musical phrase, and highly emotive with the intent of the music. Rather than this occurring in performance, some conductors choose to maximize this action in rehearsal, and minimize it in performance, the hope being that the musicality will remain intact.

Getting the Starting Pitch

If the piece is a cappella, there needs to be a plan for getting it started on pitch. The only physical thing involved here, hopefully, is the ears. A program that is well organized and running very smoothly gets a jolt if the conductor leaves the conducting location and goes to the piano to play the starting pitch. He or she then must walk back to their location and start the piece. This is amateurism at its worst.

A pitch pipe blown by the conductor is a better method. That way the conductor is in control and stays in place. If a reliable singer is willing to undertake this responsibility, they can be certain to get it right if tape is put over the holes of the pitch pipe adjacent to the desired pitch. Regardless of who offers the pitch, rehearsal practice is important so the singers are comfortable with this procedure. Many choirs do this very well—the audience takes little notice

Needless to say, this is a small but critical aspect of any a cappella performance.

Applause, the Final Bow, the Exit

Audiences like to applaud! It makes them feel they are one with the performance. They will follow cues from the conductor if there are times when they should not applaud. While still facing the choir, the conductor's left or right hand, held up at the end of a piece, will discourage applause. This is often appropriate if two or three short pieces are being performed as a group. It will help the audience understand the procedure if these pieces are clearly defined as a set in the printed program.

On occasion one sees a printed program indicate, "please, no applause until the end of the first half of the program." The audience now is left out. Perhaps there are six, or more, pieces with no applause allowed—this creates an uncomfortable, rather eerie feeling as the audience just sits there and listens—and waits to respond. It is best to bring the audience into the event. They are there to encourage the performers, and to show their appreciation.

Throughout the program, the conductor's task is to graciously receive and acknowledge applause and to recognize any special performers, inviting them to take appropriate bows. The conclusion of a concert is the time for the conductor to step aside, and let the choir be the first to acknowledge the applause, again recognizing any special performers. This all sounds quite simple on paper—and it is simple if careful planning has taken place. At the end of a symphony performance, Gustavo Dudamel, conductor of the Los Angeles Philharmonic, steps off the podium, walks forward into the orchestra, and points to special soloists, one by one, indicating they should stand; next he motions the rest of the orchestra to stand; and finally, still standing mid-orchestra, he turns to the audience to take his bow. He does this consistently. It is his special style—it shows his great appreciation of the performers, and a sense of modesty on his part.

Some choral directors rehearse the choir in a "bow as one." Others walk the length of the choir, acknowledging the singers with one arm extended in their direction. There are many variations on what can be done at the conclusion of a concert. It is good to observe others, then develop your own special plan for showing appreciation.

At a choral concert, audiences typically like to continue their applause as the singers exit—often they applaud until the very last singer is out of sight. An exit strategy needs to be rehearsed, as it is every bit as important as the entrance. It will, of necessity, vary with the venue. If the performance takes place on a stage, simply going offstage into the wings in the reverse formation of the entrance is often the only possibility. If the venue is a church with only a few steps, a procession-style exit down the center aisle works well, the singers going two-by-two, arm in arm, smiling at the audience and each other as they depart. And as suggested earlier, the singers may sing their way out. In this case the audience will be listening as they leave, not applauding, and then be left with no reason to applaud, the singers being out of sight after their exit song. The audience then stands and makes their own exit. Weather and space permitting, the singers and conductor can be waiting outside, available to greet the audience. This informal, friendly ending to a concert will be enjoyed by both performers and concert attendees.

If the concert includes a reception with the audience invited to attend, at the end of the concert an announcement to that effect by the conductor is appropriate, even if this is clearly stated in the printed program. Think like the host or hostess of a party—a verbal invitation is more personal than one printed in a program. The singers should be the first to arrive at the reception, and be there, at the ready, to greet the audience. The concert is officially over when the last guest departs.

6
The Spoken Word

Should the conductor talk to the audience?

As a young teacher, it took me fifteen years to answer this question. My conductor friends all seemed to have a firm opinion: absolutely not, or yes, by all means. Now, as someone frequently attending concerts, for some conductors who talk to the audience I say no, you should not do this. To others who talk I say great, you've got it right.

So, here is the deal. The audience is there to be entertained and, yes, enlightened. If you, as the conductor, have the ability to speak well, the ability to be heard, AND something important and enlightening to say, do so. The caveat—you have carefully planned what you are to say. Even though your delivery might be intentionally designed to seem so, this is not to be off-the-cuff stuff.

Conductors who announce the piece as the audience sits in a well-lit auditorium with a program in hand are _____. You fill in the word. Those who talk, mumbling their words, and are inaudible to most of the audience are also _____. Sadly, both happen too frequently. The result: amateurism.

Grant Gershon, conductor of the Los Angeles Master Chorale, occasionally (note: not always) picks up a handheld microphone and talks to the Disney Hall audience. This despite thorough program notes and a pre-concert informative lecture. He has something special to say. And, he wants to engage the audience, letting them know he cares about their interest in the program. Bravo, Grant Gershon. For any conductor using a microphone, test it out before the concert. Be sure you know how to use it so it allows you to be heard. All microphones are not created equal—meet the one you are to use in advance and know its peculiarities.

Some conductors cover the necessary position change of the choir by talking to the audience. This, again, needs to be structured so it adds interest to the presentation. Audiences love little personal asides. Consider the next piece on the program. If a special soloist is part of it, a word of introduction might be in order. Or, offer some interesting biographical information about the composer or poet. If the next piece is a light-hearted one, a bit of humor related to the text might set it up.

Some concerts are so formal that the insertion of talk from the conductor is out of the question. You rarely see orchestral conductors talking to an audience. There is an invisible shield between audience and conductor. The formality of the occasion allows no verbal interruption. There are certain choral concerts that have this same aura. So be it.

And so there is not a one-size-fits-all answer to the question. If the style and venue of your concert warrants it, your speaking ability is good, and you have something special to say, do so. Otherwise, it's probably best you keep quiet.

Readings at a Concert

Creative concert planning might include some special readings that add to the entertainment and enlightenment value of the program. A concert with a theme might be such a program. Or, one honoring a special composer, or one celebrating a special holiday, or commemorative of an event. The guideline is to see a specific need for this, and to have the quality of the readings, (and the reader), equal to that of the music. Otherwise the readings might end up being a boring interruption to the musical flow of the event. It is important to do nothing that will dull down a concert.

7

The Printed Program

The casual concert may not require a printed program. Instead, the conductor will announce the pieces. But most of the time, a printed program is both needed and expected. It can be simply one page, with the program title as the heading, along with the name of the featured choir and its conductor, the date, and perhaps, the location of the concert. Next, there should be a listing of the titles being performed, along with the composers and their birth years. If there is a unique performer for a piece, that too should be listed. The accompanist must be credited, perhaps at the bottom of the page, along with brief thank yous.

A more extensive printed program will list the singers by section. If it is a small, elite group, singer bios and pictures may be included. If the singers get this attention, so should the conductor and any other important participant in the program. And, if the nature of the literature warrants, there may be program notes; the texts may be included. Such a program will often have a cover page. If there is a theme, a bit of art related to it might appear on the cover.

If space allows, a printed program may include ads. It is expensive to print programs. Ads can help offset the printing cost. If including them, judicially place them so they do not intrude on the aesthetic of the program. Confine them to a back page, or to the bottom of a page that has thank yous, or credits, or lists of donors.

Important to the success of the concert are notices in the program as follows:
The taking of flash pictures during the concert is forbidden.
Recording devices of any kind are not to be used.
Please turn off cell phones.

Simply having these notices in the printed program is not sufficient. Explain the rationale behind these requests to the singers and ask that they pass the word along. Nothing is more annoying at a concert than the eager parent with flash camera in hand. The most poignant moment gets a picture taken, and the flash destroys the moment.

Regardless of the number of pages comprising the printed program, the paper should be carefully chosen. Some paper is noisier than others. Test out the paper for its sound quality. An audience rattling programs is not a good thing. Choose a paper color and ink color that can easily be read in the perhaps not-so-good light of your venue. There is nothing more frustrating than a program on dark paper in a dark room.

Appendix Two presents the layout of a FileMaker Pro database designed to help gather the information for a printed program. Each concert presents unique needs as to what should be part of the printed program. It is critical for the conductor to have an efficient means to collect information for the program and to be sure nothing important is overlooked.

8

Business Matters

The choral conductor either needs to put on a new hat and take charge of the business details that relate to the concert, or have someone else do this who is interested, capable, and reliable. However, in the end, hired or volunteer concert manager or not, everyone will look at the conductor if anything goes awry. So it is entirely up to the conductor to have all of the concert details figured out, and attended to, and then delegate appropriately.

Regardless of who is in charge, choosing a support group of excellent helpers is the first step. They, like the singers, will do what is expected of them.

Concert Assistants
Parking
If parking is going to be difficult, and especially if it will be dark, attendants should be on duty. If dark, flashlights in the hands of the attendants are a must.

Tickets and Donations
Some choirs charge for their concerts. Others do not. If tickets are part of the plan, their pre-concert sale needs to be organized, as does their sale at the concert. Some directors seek out a local business to do the pre-concert sale. Others do it via their website. At the concert, informative signs, in keeping with the advertised protocol of the concert, should be highly visible. There should be no surprises for the public. If credit cards and cash can be taken, but not checks, this should be spelled out.

For those that do not choose to sell tickets, but instead, to offer the concert for free, the donation option becomes important. The concert should advertise that donations are appreciated. And the opportunity to give them should be made highly visible, both before and after the concert. The new choir can draw an audience using this approach. Those that are highly impressed with the choir just might give a generous donation, something they would not be likely to do had they bought a ticket.

Ushers

It is advisable to schedule a meeting of the ushers as a group. They are the hosts and hostesses of the event. Their demeanor and appearance are very important to the occasion. An usher (or ushers) designated to take tickets will need to be on hand at each entrance. If there are printed programs, they should be ample in supply, and ushers need to be there to hand them out. To avoid latecomers causing a disturbance, ushers will need to be stationed at all possible entrances. They should be instructed to delay the entry of latecomers until applause between selections. If there is a side door in the venue, an usher should be nearby to deter any early departers from opening this door.

Seating

Reserving of seats is sometimes necessary for special guests. These seats need to be roped off, and ushers need to be informed of their intended use.

Sound and Recording Issues

During the concert, if amplification of any sort is needed, this should be tested in advance and ready to go.

If the concert is to be recorded, a person will be needed to place the microphones and operate the equipment. A pre-concert test during a final rehearsal is highly advisable. The same can be recommended if a video is to be made of the concert.

Today the video has a double value. First, it will provide the singers and the director with a means to evaluate the concert. Many conductors plan an after-concert viewing session for this purpose. In addition, with YouTube now all the thing, selections from the video can be posted for the world to see. Computer programs for video editing, along with video cameras with excellent sound capabilities, make it possible for the amateur videophile to achieve a fine result.

Stage Management

If the concert takes place in an auditorium, there will likely be a stage manager who comes with the territory. This person will need careful instructions as to lighting for both the stage and the auditorium. They will be in charge of all matters relating to the stage: setup of risers, use of the stage curtain, microphone needs, setup of a choral shell, and placement of decorative items. They should have a printout of the program with specific instructions as to what they are expected to do, both before and during a concert.

If the concert is in a hall or church with no stage manager, someone will need to be in charge of any setup required. If chairs and stands are needed for instrumentalists, or if something as simple as a door needs to be closed after singers enter, these details should be assigned to a helper.

Reception

If there is to be a reception after the concert, this will need to be organized. This can simply be a gathering in a space adjacent, or near the concert venue. Or it can include refreshments, and even an after-glow of entertainment. Delightful is the reception that features a solo singer, or a duet—performers entirely removed from the essence of the concert and offered as light-hearted entertainment.

Advertising the Concert

Posters, strategically placed, can be helpful in advertising the concert. The design of the poster should relate to that of the printed program. In some cities, radio announcements are possible, the station regularly announcing local concerts. The newspaper ad is another possibility. This will cost money, depending on the size of the ad and the number of times it runs. Some papers list events. Find out the deadline for getting information to the appropriate person so your concert can be included. Fliers are another option—singers can give these to their friends and they can be placed, with permission, in places such as libraries, museums, or stores. If the choir has a database of addresses of possible concert attendees, fliers also can be mailed. And, if the choir has a website, the concert details should be up front and highly visible there.

The Choir Support Group

A wonderful invention is the choir support group. For the school choir, this will no doubt be interested parents who want to be helpful. For the community, or the collegiate group, it will more likely be community people who love choral music and want to be involved. The choir support group can be looked to for all kinds of assistance. For the choir lacking a board responsible for developing ways to raise money, these people may be asked to assist in that endeavor. They also can be on duty at concerts, helping out by serving as ushers or parking attendants. They may be at a table selling CDs, T-shirts, or refreshments at intermission and after a concert. They might also be tour groupies, the first to be invited to join the choir in that adventure. And, if need be, it's possible that one of them might be interested in writing the program notes for the printed program.

Some directors recognize these people in the printed program. Others introduce them as a group at a concert. In one case, the director presents an annual trophy to the most helpful member of the support group. The director should consider these people as friends and treat them as such. Special treats are in order: a dinner at the director's home; a chance to watch a special rehearsal; an invitation to a private concert; Christmas carolers from the choir at a support group party. Nurture and treasure the help and interest of these special people.

Appreciation

After the concert, thank yous should be extended to all involved. Very important are those people associated with the venue. The fee that was paid for the privilege of using a place does not substitute for the fact that appreciation should be expressed.

9
The Concert
For a Community Group

For many choirs, it is important that they have a chance to test out their skills before getting on stage for a major concert. When seeking opportunities for singing engagements in the community, the conductor has a responsibility to their singers: to provide them with excellent performing opportunities. So it is important that the conductor be judicious as they accept or seek invitations to sing.

Good acoustics, as always, should be a primary consideration. It can be a tremendous downer for a choir to try to sing at a banquet hall completely lacking in reverb. The Santa Barbara Biltmore's large banquet hall was once a glorious place to perform. Then new owners took over and re-thought the room. They added enormous, beautiful tapestries to the walls. The acoustics now are every bit as good as a clothes closet. No longer is this an acceptable place to sing. Many hotel halls have a similar problem. The rooms are intentionally engineered to deaden sounds. Often the invitation to sing will involve such a venue—the benefit luncheon, the corporate dinner. Both frequently happen in such places.

Beyond acoustics, considerations include the type of event and the idea for the presentation. If singers are expected to be background-music, better they stay home. Invitations such as those asking them to sing while people are coming into a party should flash a red light. People come into parties talking and socializing. It's not the best time for a choir to be singing.

If the school choir is asked to sing at an assembly for their peers, the choice of song must be carefully considered. This is not the time to show off the Latin motet. It is best to pick fun pieces, a "hook" if you will. This performance just might induce some of the singers' peers to want to join the group. They can later learn to love the Latin motet.

Invitations to sing outdoors should be carefully considered. Outside, by itself, is not a good place to sing. If there is a shell, and the guarantee of amplification, it may be worth considering, particularly if the event is a worthy one.

Community service clubs are often a good source of invitations. Some of these clubs lend financial support to the arts. These groups are especially deserving of a performance.

A senior citizen facility will always welcome a performance. Many have fine pianos and good acoustic halls.

Good community public relation efforts are important for the success of any choral program. With that in mind, seek local opportunities for the singers to practice performing—and to do a group in the city a favor at the same time.

10
The Tour Concert

Things will happen on tour that would never happen at home. So it is best for the conductor to only take a choir on tour if they like adventure. Here is a little test to evaluate your touring ability:

> I have conducted successful concerts on the home front. yes or no
> I am physically fit. yes or no
> I have lots of energy. yes or no
> I love new experiences. yes or no
> I easily adapt to stressful situations. yes or no
> I am creative in thinking of solutions to problems. yes or no
> I love to travel and have done a lot of it. yes or no
> I feel able to counsel people in time of need. yes or no
> I am a strong leader and am able to enforce rules. yes or no

If no was your answer to even one of these questions, touring might not be the best for you.

Why Take a Choir on Tour?

The best answer to this is simple: singers love to go on tour. They often join choirs because a tour is part of the deal. For some singers, it will be the only time they ever get the opportunity to travel. The camaraderie of a tour group is very special, the bonding of a group on a tour is assured. As for the music, it gets better and better as opportunities are afforded daily to perform. For the conductor, it is a challenge. Can you make the tour a tremendous, special event for all involved?

The Conductor on Tour

Much of what is true about planning the home concert applies to planning the tour concert. The difference: not every detail of a concert can be anticipated when on tour. If the tour is taking you to places you have not personally experienced, you need to be prepared to be flexible and creative to deal with what you will encounter. The concert venue may be very large, but the area for the singers very small. There may be an out of tune piano, or no piano. The acoustics may be less than desirable. The possibilities for challenges are many. It is important to find out before leaving home as much as possible about both the venues and the audiences. Last-minute surprises can be difficult, or impossible, to deal with.

Many conductors never leave home without a tour director. The function of the tour director is to micro-manage all of the details of the tour. Without this person, the conductor is, like at home, responsible for everything. But now everything includes sleeping arrangements, meals, transportation, and unknown venues.

Touring with a young choir presents unique challenges. The tour should be short, the travel time short, and perhaps even the concert program should be short. In addition to the scheduled concerts, a carefully structured program of activities is a must. Having adequate adult chaperones is crucial. They will need very clear information about every detail of the tour. The chaperones will act as extensions of the conductor, their function being to help keep everything running smoothly.

The Music You Perform

Tour companies can create tours that are venue specific, i.e., the concerts will be presented only in cathedrals or great churches. This is typical of many a European tour. The literature then can easily be chosen. The only hitch might be the matter of accompaniment. The organ may be impossible to use or badly positioned. There very likely will be no piano. For this type of tour, it is best that the majority of literature be a cappella. Other pieces might feature a flute, a clarinet, or a small percussion instrument, the players traveling as part of the group.

American tour groups going to a foreign country often choose to perform something home-spun, such as a beautiful or fun folk song. They also often perform something of folk origin from the country they are visiting. Both make the performance extra special for the foreign audience.

The smart tour program has great flexibility, with several repertoire options. Arriving at a venue, the conductor needs to size it up as to what is both possible and appropriate. If there is a good piano, the piece with piano accompaniment can be performed. If not, another piece in the repertoire can substitute. If the audience is to be a young one, some pieces might be better saved for another occasion.

Since rehearsal time may be slight in the venue, it is wise to keep the mechanics of the concert fairly simple. A procession that requires careful timing may not be a good idea. The staging movement from piece to piece used at the home concert may be cumbersome in the unfamiliar venue. The conductor needs to assess the possibilities and then do whatever is necessary to ensure the best possible presentation of the music.

Impromptu singing is not unusual when on tour. The singers love to sing—given the opportunity to sing on a ferry boat ride, or in a resonant metro station, they are likely to do so. It is important that the tour repertoire include pieces that would be fun to do on occasions less formal than the scheduled concert.

The People You Take Along

Organization begins at home. The members of a tour group of any age, children through adult, need to know the rules and agree to abide by them. The tour has a singular purpose: to sing and sing well. Dedication to that purpose is a must. Here the conductor needs to rule with a tight hand. It is not without reason to have all tour participants sign an agreement contract prior to leaving home. They agree to abide by all demands of the tour. This contract should carefully spell out the expectations, rules, and details appropriate to the specific tour.

Some conductors like to take along groupies. These are often people somehow connected to the choir. Or, they may simply be people who love choral music and want to share in the experience the tour affords. It is important that these people understand the rules of the trip and agree to be helpful travelers. They too should have a contract spelling out the details of the tour and their part in it. The tour that includes extra people definitely should have a tour guide. It is way too much for any conductor to tackle responsibility for a group beyond the actual singers. That said, it is always wise to have at least one helpful outsider along. In an emergency, small or large, this person can be invaluable. Things that may happen include the lost passport, the stolen wallet, the sprained ankle, the missing shoe, the ill singer, and the home-sick singer. Any conductor who has experienced a tour knows: stuff happens.

Business Matters

Raising money for tours can be a difficult issue. Some singers can pay their own way. Others need help. Asking for money for a tour can create ill will if not done carefully. A person may respond, yes they want to go to Europe—so do I!

At Santa Barbara City College we did a thing called Rent-A-Carol. Some of the singers had part-time jobs and could earn most of their tour money by working. Others were out almost every evening in December singing for parties in the city. They went as quartets or octets, depending on the size of the occasion, wore their standard performing outfits with a touch of red added, and had a repertoire of thirty minutes of carols. The singers then each had their share of the money received credited to their tour account. This was run like a little business, including a person in charge of booking these engagements, and a November ad in the local paper. The demand grew over the years, with people calling in September to book a group for their December event.

Other groups have been seen having car washes, cookie sales at concerts, and CD sales with the profits going toward the tour. One can hope that donations would come from community groups who had been entertained by the choir, as well as from friendly donors who want to support the choir and their activities.

Some choirs charge admission for some or all of their tour concerts, thereby offsetting much of the expense of the tour. In this case, ticket sales and the collection of same are much like the business matters of an at-home concert.

If there is a printed program for a tour, it often says: "Repertoire will be chosen from the following." This allows for flexibility in fitting the program to the venue. The conductor then may need, at some point, to announce what is to be sung. Beyond listing the titles, this printed program also should include some information about the choir that would be of interest to attendees.

In some cases, the choir on tour is seen as an ambassador for a school. The private school, or the college, may cover much of the tour expense if they feel it will bring new students their way. In this case, the printed program will be obligated to include information about the school as well as the choir.

The Nature of the Tour

Not every choir will be able to take a trip to a far-off land. A tour could cover a short distance and still accomplish a great deal. A possibility for the school choir is to sing for other school choirs. Singers love to hear choirs on a personal level like this. They make exceptionally appreciative audiences when singing for each other. This can be just a musical event, or it can also be a social event that includes a meal and a time of sharing.

A tour of cities within driving distance might include home stays. Some conductors have success arranging this with both churches and schools. However, it takes a lot of work and a lot of cooperation to put this together. And one should be willing to reciprocate should the request arise.

As a conductor, my favorite tour experience was to not so far off Puerto Vallarta, Mexico, a sister city of Santa Barbara. The tour gave rise to a host of challenges that the Santa Barbara City College Chamber Singers would never be asked to deal with at home. The city fathers were the ones to come up with ideas for us. They first asked us to participate in a parade, something we wouldn't dream of doing at home. We were delighted that the narrow, cobblestone streets of this Mexican city proved to be amazingly resonant, and the people lining the streets extremely happy to see and hear us. We had taken along some fun, upbeat pieces that were parade worthy. A barbershop quartet was part of our group—they performed a song at every intersection to exuberant applause. Next we were to sing at a school. We arrived and found they had no auditorium. We were expected to sing outside. A two-story school, the upper level had a tiled walkway surrounding it, and a nice overhang roof. We sang up in a corner under the roof with the 9 to 14-year-old students, in blue and white uniforms, standing and intently listening from below in the uncovered patio. Next, there was the standing-room-only concert in the beautiful Our Lady of Guadalupe church. Now we could uncover our more precious literature: our Latin motet, our contemporary art song. And on the last night we had dinner outside at a colorful hilltop restaurant. The owner requested that the group sing something after supper. The singers sat at our long table and sang for twenty minutes. The owner then wouldn't allow us to pay for our dinner. Memorable? You bet!

If you want an extraordinary experience, put on your courageous face and take your choir on tour!

11

The Professional Conductor

It should be the goal of every conductor to think as a professional regarding all aspects of a concert. Attend choral concerts and take note of what the best, most highly respected, conductors are doing. Collect printed programs that are exemplary of good taste. Attend conventions that feature only the very best choirs. If possible, sing with a professional choir. By associating with high standards, emulating them becomes a possibility.

The First Consideration: The Music

It has been said that the professional starts where the amateur leaves off. A good professional choir is capable of reading through a large work, such as the Fauré *Requiem,* at a level that would satisfy many an amateur choir, their read-through good enough to be the final product, ready for performance. What the professional choir does after this initial reading is spend several rehearsals fine-tuning their performance. Their goal is perfection on all levels of musicality: accuracy, tone quality, expressive nuance, textual clarity, balance and blend of parts, and above all, style.

Transfer the thinking of the professional to the amateur or school choir. The singers are limited by both their ability and the expectations of the conductor. First, the ability level of the choir should be taken into careful consideration when choosing literature. It should be challenging enough to keep interest alive, but not so much so that an excellent final result is impossible to achieve. Better to do a terrific job on a moderately difficult piece than a half-way job on a very difficult one. Second, it behooves the conductor to have a musical picture in mind of exactly what the final result should be, coupled with the expertise to bring the singers up to this level. The singers will try hard to do what is expected of them. If challenged to be excellent, they will strive to do so. Accustom the singers to think as does the professional: perfection is the goal.

The Second Consideration: Everything Else

High standards should permeate everything related to a concert, not just the performance of the music. Start at the front door with the ticket taker and the usher with the printed program. Then consider the advertised starting time: programs should start on time. If for some reason there is an emergency that will cause a delay beyond a few minutes, the audience should be informed. Think through all of the details to the end of the concert. Every element needs to be carefully planned. Nothing is amateur; everything is inspired by professional standards.

The concert may have untold meaning for the singers. Years after the fact, one of them might say, "Singing in your choir was the best part of my school years." The routine rehearsal can make the day for many a singer, but when it comes to the concert, it is akin to winning the game. It is the proof of the worth of many hours of preparation. Singers will stand taller after a great concert. They will recall this concert for a lifetime.

As for the audience, people come to concerts with expectations. If their expectations are met, they are excited about what they see and hear, and they appreciate the hospitality of the event, they will be anxious to come again. They are also likely to tell others that a concert by this group is not to be missed.

May it be so!

Appendix One
The Venue Plan

Appendix 1-4 present reduced-size copies of layouts from the FileMaker Pro database titled The Concert Planner. The database is available for download at www.sbmp.com.

VENUE INFORMATION

first date of concert   [　　]   time [　　]
second date of concert   [　　]   time [　　]
third date of concert   [　　]   time [　　]
concert title [　　　　　　　　　　　　　]

venue [　　　　]   date secured [　　]
address [　　　　]   venue phone [　　]

administrator [　　]   phone/Email [　　]
custodian [　　]   phone/Email [　　]
stage manager [　　]   phone/Email [　　]
other person [　　]   phone/Email [　　]

seating capacity [　　]
parking good or bad [　　]
ticket sale onsite ok [ ] yes [ ] no
cost of venue [　　]
contract limitations [　　　　　　]

piano quality [　　]
organ quality [　　]
space for instruments [　　]
procession possibilities [　　]
balcony for audience or performance [　　]
room for warmup [　　]
secure room for belongings [　　]
reception facility [　　　　]

Appendix Two
The Printed Program Plan

Errors and omissions on a printed program are embarrassing. A database worksheet can help eliminate such problems

THE PRINTED PROGRAM WORKSHEET - 1

first date of concert ☐   time ☐

second date of concert ☐   time ☐

third date of concert ☐   time ☐

concert title ☐

venue ☐   conductor ☐

address ☐   accompanist ☐

printer deadline date ☐   date given to printer ☐

printer/phone/Email ☐

program designer ☐

program dimensions ☐   number pages ☐   cost estimate ☐

paper choice ☐

artwork ☐

names of choirs ☐

title
composer/arr/birth yr.
soloist or inst. ☐

intermission, if so, when ☐

THE PRINTED PROGRAM WORKSHEET - 2

first date of concert ☐ time ☐

second date of concert ☐ time ☐

third date of concert ☐ time ☐

concert title ☐

SINGERS

section 1	section 2	section 3	section 4

other performers   credits

thank yous

pictures

program notes

performer bios

ads   requests for audience

Appendix Three
The Business Plan

With a database worksheet, if you overlook something one year, you can enter the item into the database and take comfort knowing that it is there for next year.

THE BUSINESS PLAN WORKSHEET

first date of concert [   ]   time [   ]

second date of concert [   ]   time [   ]

third date of concert [   ]   time [   ]

concert title [   ]

deadline dates...   ticket prices [   ]
secure venue [   ]
program to printer
flier, tickets to printer
concert helpers notified

ticket sales arrangements [   ]
before concert

ticket sales arrangements [   ]
at the concert

flier designed ☐ yes ☐ no   newspaper ad ☐ yes ☐ no

tickets designed ☐ yes ☐ no   choir website ad ☐ yes ☐ no

radio ad arranged ☐ yes ☐ no   local concert listings ☐ yes ☐ no

                                      instrument parts in hand ☐ yes ☐ no

ushers [   ]
name/phone/Email

parking attendants [   ]
name/phone/Email

reception helpers [   ]
name/phone/Email

other non-choir [   ]
participants notified
name/phone/Email

comp tickets set aside [   ]
recipient names

Appendix Four
Evaluate the Concert

We are all learning in this business. Take time to reflect after a concert and give yourself pointers for next time.

CONCERT EVALUATION

first date of concert [   ] time [   ]
second date of concert [   ] time [   ]
third date of concert [   ] time [   ]
concert title [   ]

ticket sales
1st
2nd
3rd
total

venue evaluation

audience response

performer response

newspaper review

other

Appendix Five
Choristers and Other Critters

The process whereby a thematic program is born is not one that can be "cornered." The possibilities for inspiration are endless. When contacted for some input on programs she had presented, Anna Hamre responded with three program titles, the last of which was "Choristers and Other Critters." Curious myself, and not wanting to leave anyone wondering what in the world this was all about, I asked her to clue us in on what was going on here. She responded saying this was one of her favorite programs, and sent along what you see below. Enjoy!

Lizards?
Initially I had trouble bonding with a text about lizards. Our percussion instructor, Matthew Darling, returned from a sabbatical carrying G. Bradley Bodine's *Desert Songs,* a multi-movement work for SATB choir, soprano soloist, two percussionists, and an ocean of instruments and noise-makers.

We agreed on the second movement that sang about coyotes, crickets, mice, cactus wrens, and lizards. Given the heft of the work, it needed to be the concert closer.

Building the rest of the concert was a challenge because the school calendar dictated that this performance include a variety of ensembles, and that it happen on a date when the second percussionist could attend. Variety in this concert would not be a problem; unity would be a challenge.

I landed on the title "Choristers and Other Critters," to which the percussionists objected. "Oh great," they moaned, "we're the critters?!"

Starting with a potpourri of music the students needed to perform for educational reasons, the concert progressed to the second segment: "A Counterpoint of Other Species." (The pun on species counterpoint was for the composition majors.) Selections included such pieces as *Kde Sú Krávy Moje (Where are my cows?)* by H. A. Schimmerling, *Abschiedslied der Zugvögel (Farewell Song of the Birds)* by Felix Mendelssohn, a setting of the American folksong *The Cuckoo*, and *The Silver Swan* by Orlando Gibbons. We placed ensembles in different locations in the hall to present short, light-hearted works without pause, including pieces like Josquin dez Pres' *El Grillo (The Cricket)*. Some music-education students were assigned segments from Carolyn Jennings delightful children's set of animal songs. The choreographed *Whale* was particularly memorable.

But the hit of the evening was *Desert Songs II*, a fine piece of music. The work (listed at www.gbradleybodine.com) requires professional-level percussionists, along with a soprano soloist who wails in an uncanny representation of a coyote howling. And the lizard part turned out pretty well, too.

Anna Hamre
Director of Choral Activities, Fresno State University

End note from the author:
A program title discovered at composer Bradley's website:
From Bach to Bodine with Broadway in Between.

Appendix Six
Repertoire Information

The titles listed were referred to in the book. Complete scores and recordings are available for reference at www.sbmp.com.

SBMP 557 Alleluia, René Clauson, SATB div., a cappella

SBMP 707 Alleluia, Terry Schlenker, SATB div., a cappella

SBMP 54 Alleluia, Rejoice! J. Edmund Hughes, SATB, handbells

SBMP 516 Alleluia, Rejoice! J. Edmund Hughes, TB, handbells

SBMP 881 Alleluyah Sasa, Ben Allaway, SATB div., a cappella (percussion)

SBMP 781 Animalia, Earl J. Reisdorff, unison, piano

SBMP 66 Bandari, Ben Allaway, SATB div., a cappella (percussion)

SBMP 814 Dancing Tree, Nancy Gifford , SA, piano, flute

SBMP 67 Freedom Come, Ben Allaway, SATB, congas

SBMP 68 Freedom Come, Ben Allaway, TTBB, congas

SBMP 133 Freedom Come, Ben Allaway, SSAA, congas

SBMP 223 How Can I Keep from Singing, arr. Neil Ginsberg, SSA, piano

SBMP 407 How Can I Keep from Singing, arr. Scott Farthing, SSA, piano

SBMP 408 How Can I Keep from Singing, arr. Scott Farthing, TTB, piano

SBMP 894 How Can I Keep from Singing, arr. Karen P. Thomas, SSAA, a cappella

SBMP 897 How Can I Keep from Singing, arr. Karen P. Thomas, SATB, a cappella

SBMP 859 How Can I Keep from Singing, David Bridges, SSA, piano *

SBMP 540 The Moon Is Distant from the Sea, David N. Childs, SATB, piano

SBMP 719 The Moon Is Distant from the Sea, David N. Childs, SSAA, piano

SBMP 764 The Moon Is Distant from the Sea, David N. Childs, TTBB, piano

SBMP 137 Pentatonic Alleluia, Ross Whitney, SA, a cappella

SBMP 444 Pentatonic Alleluia, Ross Whitney, SSAATBB, a cappella

SBMP 927 The Poem, the Song, the Picture, Terry Schlenker, SATB div., a cappella

SBMP 951 The Poem, the Song, the Picture, Terry Schlenker, SSAA, a cappella

SBMP 728 Rejoice! Jeffery L. Ames, SATB, piano

SBMP 431 With a Lily in Your Hand, Eric Whitacre, SATB, a cappella

SBMP 938 Wondrous Love, arr. Kevin S. Foster, SSATB, a cappella

* SBMP 859 is set to an original melody, not the familiar one

Appendix Seven
The Database

As a choral conductor working mainly in the pre-digital age, I did not have the advantage of a database to keep me organized. Instead, I saved programs and reviews, storing them in a filing cabinet, and each year made a list of ideas for the following year. If the need arose to find the name of the fabulous flutist in a long-ago program, I would need to dig through a tall pile of papers hoping to eventually find the name.

With a searchable database one can quickly bring to light any item of stored information. Cut a finger on a rusty nail and your medical records can tell you when you last had a tetanus shot. If you are a cook, you can enter, and forever refer to, all of your lasagna recipes. If you compose, you can keep track of your submissions to publishers and hopefully the royalty receipts. For your residence, you can access your household maintenance database and know which plumber to call. The possibilities are endless. FileMaker Pro offers templates ready-to-go for all kinds of uses. However, none are specifically for the choral conductor. The two databases offered here have been created to fill that need.

At *www.sbmp.com* the Personal Choral Library database can be downloaded for free. The Concert Planner Database is available for $10.

As is typical of any computer program, FileMaker Pro continually has upgrades. As of this 2011 writing it is available as follows:

> FileMaker Pro 11 for Mac or PC: $299
> The same program at the Academic Superstore:
>   student or teacher price $177

The program can be had on a free 30-day trial basis. Visit the FileMaker Pro website for the latest product information.

About the Author

Barbara Harlow has directed choirs at all levels, elementary through college. At a junior high school, her teaching assignment included two choirs; at a high school, five; and at a community college, three. During her thirteen-year tenure at Santa Barbara City College, her choirs presented concerts at the Santa Barbara Mission and two Catholic churches; at three Protestant churches and the Unitarian Society; in two school auditoriums, and at the college campus center. Her choirs performed at numerous social occasions in various banquet halls in the greater Santa Barbara area. And her Chamber Singers toured to Mexico, Europe, Canada, and throughout California.

A four-year scholarship recipient and *cum laude* graduate of the University of Southern California, she has a master's degree in composition from California State University at Fullerton. She is the author of a textbook for community college voice classes, *You, the Singer* published by Hinshaw Music, and *How to Get Your Choral Composition Published,* a publication of Santa Barbara Music Publishing. She sang professionally with the Roger Wagner Chorale, and in addition to conducting choirs, has taught voice, piano, guitar, and music theory. In 1990, after taking an early retirement from teaching, she established Santa Barbara Music Publishing.

Below is a review of one of her many Santa Barbara choral concerts:

> The Christmas season arrived in Santa Barbara a bit early last night with the first of two presentations of a "Christmas Carol Dinner Concert," by the Santa Barbara City College Chamber Singers, at the Montecito Country Club.
>
> This is the first time the group has done a dinner concert off campus, and as director Barbara Harlow told last night's thrilled and uplifted audience at the close of the program, she chose the main dining room at the country club because it is "one of the best sounding rooms in the city."
>
> The 22 members of the Chamber Singers were in wonderful voice, providing a rich, emotional experience that brought tears to the eyes of several in the audience. The acoustics are wonderful, and the singers took full advantage of the cozy, candlelit room, singing from a balcony, or standing in a group, or scattered all around the room, surrounding the audience with beautiful sounds. Unfortunately, all tickets have been sold for tonight's second and final performance.
>
> *Bob Barber, Santa Barbara Newspress*